T0064179

mentoring. It's 4 uMom is a fresh opportunity for this type of camaraderie. It exhibits women journeying together as mothers and wives, seeking after God's heart for the sake of their families. The beauty of Titus 2 is played out for mothers of all ages, and the Lord is glorified!

Kim Dal Porto, MD
Carithers Pediastrics
Jacksonville, Florida

"I would highly recommend inserting "It's 4 U Mom" into your church outreach program. We recently started it here at Fellowship, and have already seen results. God's Hand of blessing is on this outreach ministry, born in the heart of Josie Aenis, who not only understands the day to day struggles women face, but she also understands how to reach out to them in a unique way. "It's 4 U Mom" is an exciting, inviting way for your church to reach out to women in your local community."

Cheryl Grover
Pastor's Wife
Fellowship Baptist Church
Thonotosassa, Florida

As the featured speaker at two of the "mom's events" Josie Aenis planned and hosted, I witnessed firsthand how well-organized, Christ-centered, and welcoming the events were to the women in the community. I was impressed with the attention to specific details, which resulted in the events flowing smoothly in a relaxed, upbeat atmosphere. The obvious focal point of all that transpired during the events was to encourage every woman in attendance.

Pam Tebow
Mother of five
Professional speaker

....

It is with great joy that I recommend 4uMoms by Mrs. Josie Aenis. I have known her and the family for over a quarter of a century. "Wisdom is justified of her children"; her family is her best recommendation.

Solomon also gives her a good word when he describes her with the words, "[s]he that winneth souls is wise." Josie is the best lady soul-winner I have met in my 48 years of ministry.

Dr. Charles Keen
Founder of First Bible International
Milford, Ohio

....

For several years Josie Aenis led our preschool ministry here at Trinity Baptist Church and through her experience developed the program, "It's 4 U Mom," which has been a huge success in our ministry.

The program is effective in helping to reach mothers and connect them to healthy ministry and mentors. I highly recommend the program and am grateful for the passion and energy that Josie brings to helping women in ministry.

In His Service,
Tom Messer
Senior Pastor
Trinity Baptist Church
Jacksonville, Florida

....

"I have read with interest and delight Josie Aenis' helpful Manual, "It's 4 uMom." Having spoken in well over 400 local churches, I can attest that there is a great need for this ministry in churches everywhere. It is practical, proven, and Biblical!

Charles T. Shoemaker, Ed.D.
President, Church Planting America

....

As a private pediatrician and mother of a blended family of six children, I strongly endorse a program for moms to receive spiritual insight and inspiration, encouraging fellowship, and

It's 4 uMom

Building Relationships through Every Stage of Mothering

Josie Aenis

WESTBOW
PRESS
A DIVISION OF THOMAS NELSON
& ZONDERVAN

Copyright © 2015 Josie Aenis.

All rights reserved. No part of this book may be used or reproduced by any means, graphic, electronic, or mechanical, including photocopying, recording, taping or by any information storage retrieval system without the written permission of the author except in the case of brief quotations embodied in critical articles and reviews.

Scripture taken from the King James Version of the Bible.

Copyright 1985 C.D. Stanley Enterprises. In.

WestBow Press books may be ordered through booksellers or by contacting:

WestBow Press
A Division of Thomas Nelson & Zondervan
1663 Liberty Drive
Bloomington, IN 47403
www.westbowpress.com
1 (866) 928-1240

Because of the dynamic nature of the Internet, any web addresses or links contained in this book may have changed since publication and may no longer be valid. The views expressed in this work are solely those of the author and do not necessarily reflect the views of the publisher, and the publisher hereby disclaims any responsibility for them.

Any people depicted in stock imagery provided by Thinkstock are models, and such images are being used for illustrative purposes only.
Certain stock imagery © Thinkstock.

ISBN: 978-1-4908-8863-7 (sc)
ISBN: 978-1-4908-8864-4 (e)

Print information available on the last page.

WestBow Press rev. date: 08/11/2015

Contents

Preface

It's 4 uMom is a community-outreach program. As children of God, our joy, our enthusiasm, and our delight in life come alive when we see individuals come to know Christ as their personal Savior.

Being a mom, kindergarten teacher, day-care administrator, and grandmother, I have seen firsthand the balancing act moms are involved in and the encouragement and support they need daily.

A few years ago, I had the privilege of starting a moms' group at our church. This meant we had to reach out into the community to invite moms to our campus. We invited speakers of interest to these community moms, including pediatricians; financial consultants; well-known moms, such as Pam Tebow; local TV anchors; and police officers, talking about safety issues.

Throughout the past eight years of hosting these moms' groups, we have built long-lasting relationships with moms in the community. We have had the thrill of leading more than thirty-five adults to the Lord as a result of this community-outreach ministry. By inviting, being a friend, and building relationships, we can win them. It works! Try it, and see how this particular outreach ministry will bring enthusiasm, enjoyment, and delight to your congregation as you connect with community moms and their families.

Mission Statement

It's 4 uMom believes in building relationships with community moms through avenues of interest and concerns moms face daily. Meetings have special speakers—for example, a pediatrician, an executive chef, or a financial consultant. It can also be an evening of sitting and connecting with each other. Women have opportunities to show Christ's love through their inner actions with their new friends. In return, moms come to know Christ, and the Spirit of God draws the family to believe as well. This is based on Acts 16:31: "And they said, Believe on the Lord Jesus Christ and thou shalt be saved, and thy house" (King James Version).

It's 4 uMom believes that with prayer and direction from the Holy Spirit, this outreach endeavor can be implemented through the church and can build relationships in the community. There will be eternal results for God's glory.

It's 4 uMom welcomes you to a new method of reaching people for Christ.

Statement of Faith

It's 4 uMom is a Christian outreach organizational ministry. It gives churches opportunities to adapt this new method within their outreach programs and connect with community families for Christ.

It's 4 uMom believes in the Gospel of Jesus Christ—His death, burial, resurrection, and return.

It's 4 uMom believes Jesus Christ is the only way to heaven, and believing in His name, one may have eternal life.

It's 4 uMom believes in the Bible as the inspired, God-breathed Word, and the foundation of the Gospel truth.

It's 4 uMom believes in the deity of God the Father, Son, and Holy Spirit.

It's 4 uMom believes in order to fulfill Acts 1:8 ("But ye shall receive power after that the Holy Ghost is come upon you: and ye shall be witnesses unto me both in Jerusalem, and in all Judaea, and in Samaria, and unto the uttermost part of the earth" [King James Version]), we need to be busy in "our Jerusalem" and reach the people around us.

Overview

Building Relationships through Every Stage of Mothering

The Purpose: Reaching the community by reaching moms

The Tool: It's 4 uMom

It's 4 uMom is dependent on the following leadership positions:

1. The Pastor: The pastor of the local church must be behind this outreach 100 percent for this program to be implemented successfully.

2. Director: The director oversees the outreach program.

3. Coordinator: The coordinator leads the team of volunteer supervisors.

4. It's 4 uKids Supervisor: This supervisor oversees child care.

5. Hospitality Supervisor: This supervisor is responsible for greeting guests and providing refreshments.

6. Publicity Supervisor: This supervisor is responsible for advertising.

7. Table Supervisors: These supervisors connect the community mom with the church.

8. Mentor Mom(s): These moms give wisdom, insight, and prayer for the younger moms.

It's 4 uMom is an outreach opportunity for your church to develop relationships with moms in your community, to help meet their needs, and to show them the love of Christ.

Getting Started

Description of It's 4 uMom Outreach Program

It's 4 uMom is an outreach program to assist the local church in a new endeavor of community outreach. The charter church may take the logo and the yearly theme and adapt the meetings to fit their church environment.

Steps to Starting an It's 4 uMom Outreach Program

❑ Meet with the pastor of the church. Where, what, when, and why should the church start this outreach ministry? Who is willing to help with this outreach? Where would the group meet? When would they meet (morning or evening meetings)? Would child care be provided and for what ages? How would this outreach be funded?

❑ Meet with women leaders in the church. These can be women with expertise in certain areas of this ministry, including those with coordinating, publicity, hospitality, and child-care skills. It would include mature mothers to mentor younger ones and young moms to serve as table leaders.

❑ Implement a financial budget (see appendix for a sample budget).

❑ Designate leadership responsibilities (see appendix for leadership hierarchy and organizational time line for each leader).

❑ Meet with supervisors in leadership.

  – Pray for guidance, attendees, and scheduling of the meetings.

  – Discuss the steps and ideas to fit the desire of the charter church or organization: location and time of meeting, child care, decorations, supplies, speakers, advertisement, finances, and so on.

To the Director of It's 4 uMom

- The pastor of the charter church must approve the It's 4 uMom outreach program.

- The group that uses It's 4 uMom must be financially supported by the church or have a plan to budget the needs within the group.

  Options:

  1. The church pays for the advertising and use of materials for the It's 4 uMom group and for an honorarium to guest speakers.

  2. The church charges the women who attend each meeting. The fee would start at $1.00 and increase as necessary. It would pay for door prizes, refreshments for the women, and refreshments and crafts for child care.

- The director presents outreach to all women members of the church.

- The director will arrange for the following for general meetings:

  1. a designated coordinator, hospitality supervisor, It's 4 uKids supervisor, publicity supervisor, table supervisor, and mentor mom

  2. a decorated meeting room (atmosphere and climate are essential to success; budgeting required)

  3. crafts for children and moms (optional)

Basic Timeline for It's 4 uMom

The following timeline is vital for having a successful program. Following this timeline will help organizers make certain all responsibilities are accomplished in a timely manner and not left to a last-minute rush.

☐ 3–4 Months Prior to the First Meeting

1. The director will meet with the women of the church and present the outreach ministry.

2. Decide when meetings will take place, day or evening, based on the church calendar. Meeting twice a month allows relationships to develop.

3. Designate a coordinator and supervisors. The director assigns these positions according to talent, abilities, and availability.

4. The coordinator assigns responsibilities to supervisors. (Handouts of guidelines and responsibilities will be given.)

5. The director meets with all leaders to discuss the yearly theme.

   - ideas for speakers: pediatricians, police officers, executive chefs, financial consultants, fashion designer, an aesthetician, teacher

   - ideas for activities: Christmas party for moms, fashion show, couponing, mall madness (exchange items: children's clothing, house decorations, etc.), "Amazing Race" for moms, cookout, award night (perfect attendance, award caregivers, etc.)

☐ 2 Months Prior to First Meeting

1. Coordinator selects the table leaders.

   - The number of table leaders depends on size and interest of program.

   - Supervisors can be table leaders.

2. Coordinator meets with all leaders to hear reports on status of tasks.

☐ 1 Month Prior to First Meeting

1. Director meets with all leaders to hear status reports on tasks.

2. Director prays with all leaders.

   - Pray for speaker.
   - Pray for volunteers caring for children.
   - Pray for the moms attending the meeting.

☐ 2 Weeks Prior to First Meeting

1. All leaders meet to review responsibilities.

2. Responsibilities should be completed according to time frame.

3. All leaders meet to pray for the meeting.

☐ 3–4 Days Prior to Each Meeting:

1. Director/coordinator contacts all leaders.

   - phone, e-mail, or Facebook to finalize responsibilities of each position
   - help with any unfinished tasks

2. Director/coordinator contacts speaker to confirm last-minute details.

☐ Day of Each Meeting

1. Director/coordinator contacts

   - the speaker if necessary (to confirm transportation arrangements, directions, etc.);
   - the It's 4 uKids supervisor to make sure all child caregivers will be on time for child care; and
   - the hospitality supervisor to make sure food items and supplies have or are being delivered so setup is on schedule

2. Director/coordinator reviews

   - the schedule for each particular meeting and
   - items for the meeting.

3. Director/coordinator reminds

   - all leaders to be twenty to thirty minutes early and
   - all other volunteers to be fifteen minutes early.

4. Get ready to greet, meet, and build relationships.

5. Enjoy your evening.

☐ After Each Meeting

1. All leaders help with cleanup.

2. All leaders review the meeting.

Director

Description

The director must be a Christian mom and a member of the charter church. She should be faithful and loyal to the church, must have the capacity to lead others, and must have a desire for moms to grow in their relationship with God. This person must have a pleasant personality, a passion for souls, and the gift for caring and helping women in their daily lives. She must have a consistent walk with the Lord.

Responsibilities

1. Meet with coordinator about the group goals.

2. Attend group meetings directed by the coordinator.

3. Assist in getting speakers for the meetings that should coincide with the group theme for the year.

4. Pray for the group and the goals of the group.

5. Assist with decisions: meeting time and location.

6. Assist with getting door prizes. Many businesses may donate gift certificates and prizes. Prepare a letter to businesses asking for door prizes and gift certificates. The director may designate one individual in the group to handle the door prizes.

7. Assist in maintaining the overall budget.

Timeline for Director

The timeline for this position is vital to the success of this ministry. It helps the individual to be organized so things can be accomplished in a timely manner. By following the timeline, a person can stay on course and focus on having successful meetings.

☐ 3–4 Months Prior to the First Meeting

1. Meets with ladies of the church and presents the outreach ministry

2. Selects a God-gifted coordinator

3. Appoints God-gifted supervisors

4. Meets with coordinator and supervisors to discuss the following:

   - yearly theme
   - speakers for the year
   - schedule for and contact of speakers
   - responsibilities of appointed positions

5. Prays for leaders, speakers, and moms who will be attending the meetings

6. Keeps communication open to all leaders

☐ 2 Months Prior to the First Meeting

1. Contacts coordinator about progress of the supervisors' responsibilities

2. Assists where needed to help with responsibilities

3. Prays for this outreach ministry

☐ 1 Month Prior to the First Meeting

1. Meets with coordinator and supervisors to check updated reports for the meeting

2. Prays for all the leaders and their responsibilities

☐ 2 Weeks Prior to the First Meeting

1. Meets with coordinator and leaders to do the following:

   - check the reports completed by leaders
   - give assistance where needed to leaders
   - pray for all speakers, moms, and leaders

2. Checks with speaker about needs for the meeting:

   - computer/laptop for PowerPoint presentations
   - screen
   - handouts to be copied

3. Checks with designated person from the church about technical equipment needed for the meeting:

   - microphones
   - screens
   - laptop
   - air-conditioning or heat

☐ 3–4 Days Prior to Each Meeting

1. Meets with coordinator to discuss completion of all responsibilities
2. Contacts the speaker to confirm details of items needed for the meeting

☐ Day of Each Meeting

1. Contacts coordinator to confirm the completion of responsibilities of supervisors

2. Prays for the details of the meeting

3. Arrives thirty minutes before meeting

4. Greets speaker and moms as they arrive at the meeting; very important to have leaders greet moms individually to prevent group discussions among themselves and lose focus on the guests entering the room.

☐ After Each Meeting

1. Thanks the speaker and moms for attending the meeting

2. Helps with cleanup

3. Discusses with the leaders the results of the meeting

Coordinator

Description

The coordinator must be a Christian mom who is a member of the charter church and possesses the capacity to lead others. She must have the desire for moms to grow in a relationship with God. She must have skills to lead, direct, inspect, and assist the supervisors with their responsibilities. An outgoing personality and a spirit-filled life are vital for this position. It is important to have the skills to make a visitor feel welcome, important, and comfortable in her surroundings.

Responsibilities

- provide accountability to the individual supervisors

- schedule and communicate meeting times with the group supervisors

- start the It's 4 uMom meetings

- introduce the speakers

- close the meetings

- pray for the group supervisors and moms who attend

- answer to the director of the It's 4 uMom outreach program

Timeline for Coordinator

A timeline is a vital part to having a successful meeting. It helps an individual to accomplish responsibilities in a timely manner. It helps a person focus on the tasks before her. The coordinator will be better able to assist other leaders in their responsibilities if she is on time with her duties.

☐ 3–4 Months Prior to the First Meeting

1. Meets with the director to assist with the following:

   - selecting God-gifted supervisors
   - discussing theme of the year and dates and times of meetings
   - discussing supervisor's responsibilities

2. Contacts speaker and technology department (optional with director) about upcoming meeting

☐ 2 Months Prior to the First Meeting

With the assistance of the director, appoints table leaders, who may also be supervisors

☐ 1 Month Prior to the First Meeting

1. Meets with director to write up schedule of meeting (see sample in manual)

2. Meets with supervisors to review progress of responsibilities and assist where needed

3. Prays with all leaders

☐ 3–4 Days Prior to Each Meeting

1. Contacts director and reviews schedule of the meeting

2. Contacts supervisors to see that all responsibilities are complete

☐ Day of Each Meeting

1. Contacts director and gives final report of completion of responsibilities.

2. Arrives thirty minutes before meeting begins to make sure everything is ready for the meeting, last-minute details are complete, and there is time to relax before the first person arrives.

3. Greets moms as they arrive. Each leader greeting the moms should greet them separately, not in a group so the focus will be on the women entering. It is best that the leaders spread throughout the room to greet all the women.

☐ After Each Meeting:

1. Thanks the speaker for coming

2. Thanks all moms as a group and individually for coming

3. Helps with cleanup

4. Meets with all leaders to discuss results of the meeting

5. Prays with leaders

It's 4 uKids Supervisor

Description

The It's 4 uKids supervisor must be a Christian mom, a member of the charter church, and a gifted communicator with children. This woman must have some teaching experience with children. Loving children must be a prerequisite, as well as being attentive to their needs. Years of experience working with children and having an excellent record on behalf of children will help make this part of the ministry successful.

Responsibilities

1. Assists in the decision of the age group of children that are in her care.

2. Oversees the It's 4 uKids volunteers and determines if the group wants to pay the caregivers (and, if so, how much)

3. Follows the ratio of number of children to number of caregivers according to the state guidelines and church nursery and children's ministry policies

4. Oversees the schedule of the children, including the following:

   - story time

   - craft time

   - playtime

   - snack time

5. Prays for the children in her care (The children can be the entrance to connecting with the heart of the parents and reaching them for Christ.)

Timeline for It's 4 uKids Supervisor

A timeline is very important for this position. It helps an individual complete responsibilities in a timely manner. When caregivers are ready and supplies and crafts are organized for the children, it makes for a successful experience for all concerned. It makes for a less stressful environment, and that is a great goal to accomplish.

☐ 3–4 Months Prior to the First Meeting

1. 1. Meets with child-care volunteers (teenage girls, single women, older women, and couples) and does the following:

    - gives handouts with information on how the children will spend their time

    - gives handouts of responsibilities and guidelines for those involved in child care (follow the guidelines of the charter church)

2. Oversees curriculum and theme for the kids' program

3. Oversees the supplies needed for the kids' program

☐ 1 Month Prior to the First Meeting

1. Meets with child-care volunteers and designates responsibilities:

    - assigns volunteers to babies, toddlers 2–5 years old

    - assigns volunteers to school-age children

    - assigns volunteers to crafts

    - assigns volunteers to refreshments

    - assigns volunteers to story time (this person may also be a volunteer worker in a room)

2. Meets with coordinator and director to decide the age limit for child care (school-age children). (This will be determined in part by number of volunteer staff, facilities, and church policy.)

☐ 3–4 Days Prior to Each Meeting

1. Makes contact and follows up with the following:

   - volunteers and their needs
   - volunteers and their supplies for stories and crafts
   - volunteers and setup and cleanup of rooms
   - volunteers and refreshments needed

2. Makes contact with coordinator or director about any needs she may have for the It's 4 uKids program: for example, craft items, refreshments, etc.

☐ Day of Each Meeting

1. Arrives thirty minutes to an hour before the uKids program starts and does the following:

   - sees that rooms are set up and ready to go (she has volunteers scheduled to help with rooms; see section under "3–4 Days Prior")
   - sees that sign-up and ID information is ready
   - sees that stories, crafts, and refreshments are ready

2. Greets the volunteers as they arrive fifteen to twenty minutes early

3. Greets parents and children as they arrive

4. Makes sure everything begins on time

5. Checks all rooms to see that all is well and assists where needed

6. Helps the volunteers to make the program a wonderful experience for children and moms

☐ After Each Meeting

1. Has all caregivers say their good-byes to the children and moms

2. Meets to discuss how the program went

3. Makes sure all workers help clean up rooms

4. Has prayer with all workers

Child-Care Volunteers for It's 4 uKids

A caregiver's duty is to love and care for the child in the absence of his or her mom. Caregivers are to greet, meet, and care for the needs of each child who enters the room. They are to care for the child in the following ways:

1. Socially and Emotionally: Help the child adjust to surroundings and other children.

2. Physically: Change diapers or assist the child at bathroom time. Give them snacks and help with age-appropriate crafts.

3. Spiritually: Love the children, interact with them, and demonstrate compassion. Share songs and Bible stories. Pray with them. Be positive with all children.

Responsibilities

The supervisor will make certain child-care volunteers follow the guidelines of the charter church.

1. The charter church may use the guidelines of the It's 4 uKids program if they do not have child-care guidelines.

   - Use two volunteers per room of children or follow this ratio:

     – newborn–18 months—1:4 teacher/child ratio

     – 19–24 months—1:8 teacher/child ratio

     – 25–35 months—1:8 teacher/child ratio

     – 36 months–4 years—1:12 teacher/child ratio

     – 4–5 years—1:18 teacher/child ratio

     – school age—1:24 teacher/child ratio

   - These two volunteers should be women and/ or teenage girls.

   - A husband may work in a room with his wife if there is a female volunteer in the room as well. Men may hold a baby to give it a bottle or rock it to sleep. Men should not hold a toddler or older child. They may get down at their level and assist them in their activities.

- For protection and safety of children, husbands, and the church, only female volunteers can change diapers or take children to the bathroom.

1. Attend a child-care meeting with the child-care supervisor before the It's 4 uKids program begins.

2. Receive the dates and schedule of the program.

3. Women may be talented in different areas of service. Allow them to select their expertise (e.g., storytelling, snacks, etc.).

4. Love children and make sure child-care volunteers do as well.

5. Communicate with parents in a friendly and positive manner.

Child-Care Schedule

This schedule may be adjusted to meet the needs of the group.

20–30 Minutes Prior: Volunteers arrive at assigned rooms.

Start on Time: Supervisor and Volunteers

  1. Greet children and moms.

  2. Direct moms and children to age-appropriate rooms.

  3. Give moms ID card or badge for picking up child, or follow the church security system.

15 Minutes: Free play

20 Minutes: Snack time (type of food depends on time of day for this program)

15–20 Minutes: Restroom time or diaper changing

10 Minutes: Story time (length of time varies with age group)

15 Minutes: Playground time/game time in rooms

15–20 Minutes: Craft time

15 Minutes: Review of story and free play until pick-up time

School-Age Schedule

This schedule is for ages kindergarten and up for an It's 4 uKids evening program. This time allotment may be adjusted to the group's needs.

1. Supervisor will have the child-care volunteers follow the guidelines of the children's programs of the chartered church.

2. Supervisor and the charter church may follow the guidelines of It's 4 uKids if they do not have guidelines (section 3 of "Child-Care Volunteers").

3. Supervisor will allow parents and children to bring appropriate table games, hand games, and homework.

15–20 Minutes: Play time (with table games or hand games from home or from charter church)

15–20 Minutes: Homework time or free time

15–20 Minutes: Refreshment time (may vary with timing of program or may change with homework time slot)

10–15 Minutes: Restroom break

15–20 Minutes: Bible lesson

10–15 Minutes: Craft time

Chill time and dismissal

Hospitality Supervisor

Description

The hospitality supervisor must be a Christian mom, a member of the charter church, and someone who enjoys engaging in new relationships with people and hosting new moms. She should have an outgoing, sweet spirit, and she should be gifted with creative abilities.

Responsibilities

1. Greet guests as they arrive for the meeting. It is important to have the leaders greet the guests separately and not as a group. Someone can be at the entrance to the room and another at the registration table to greet the guests. Other leaders can be spread throughout the room to greet all the women before the meeting begins.

2. Oversee and make sure refreshments are provided for the meetings.

   - Ask each lady to provide some type of food.

3. The church would provide the refreshments, such as paper goods, drinks, some appetizers, and meat dishes for special meetings such as a Christmas party, or a celebration cake for award night at the end of the year.

4. Assist in making reminder calls, sending cards, or other means of communication to keep in touch with moms attending the meetings.

Timeline for Hospitality Supervisor

A timeline for this individual is very important to make sure items have been selected, purchased at great prices, and will best reflect the theme and accent of the meeting and the children's program. This timeline is to prevent the rush of last-minute plans and decisions.

☐ 3–4 Months Prior to the First Meeting

Attends all meetings that are specified for the leaders of It's 4 uMom (There will be various types of moms' meetings—such as Christmas parties, Valentine parties, and cookouts—and the menu will have to be discussed.)

☐ 1 Month Prior to the First Meeting

1. Oversees purchase of the supplies needed for the moms' meeting and for the children's program, including the following:

   - paper goods
   - decorations

2. Oversees purchase of the refreshments needed for the moms' meeting and for the children's program

   - Ladies will be assigned to bring something.
   - Church or organization will provide something.

☐ 2 Weeks Prior to the First Meeting

1. Verifies that supplies have been purchased for the upcoming event

   - Selects a date for purchase of items if needed
   - Selects a date for receipts of purchase to be given to designated person

2. Decides the location where supplies will be stored

☐ 3–4 Days Prior to Each Meeting

1. Supervisor or designated person delivers supplies to the meeting area

2. Reports to the coordinator that supplies and refreshments are ready

☐ Day of Each Meeting

1. A designated person assists with setting up of refreshments and decorations

2. Informs the coordinator of the cuisine for the next meeting

   ▪ Each woman may provide the food.

   ▪ Church or organization may provide the food.

3. Greets moms as they arrive (It is very important leaders greet guests separately, rather than stand in a group to greet guests, so they focus on the arrival of the moms entering the room.)

☐ After Each Meeting

1. Thanks the women for coming and invites them back for the next meeting

2. Assists in cleanup after the meeting

Publicity Supervisor

Description

The publicity supervisor must be a Christian mom and a member of the charter church, and ideally she has influence in the community or understands the importance of positive influence and building relationships. Someone with advertising skills, secretarial experience, or computer technology would be ideal for this position.

Responsibilities

1. Oversee advertising for the group:

   - put up posters after receiving permission from the businesses
   - contact parent magazines
   - contact libraries and doctors' and dentists' offices
   - coordinate mass mailings
   - distribute flyers in subdivisions

2. Oversee the team newsletter (optional). Newsletter ideas:

   - list community events and free activities
   - recipes, crafts to do with kids, fun games, etc.
   - thought for the week
   - home tips, cleaning the house, taking stains out of clothes, doing homework with the children, planting flowers, etc.

Timeline for Publicity Supervisor

Timing is everything for this supervisor. Advertising and announcements of meetings must be done in plenty of time so busy moms can plan accordingly. A schedule helps this individual get information out in plenty of time.

☐ 3–4 Months Prior to the First Meeting

1. Attends required meetings as designated by the director or coordinator

2. Contacts publicity agencies and businesses for promoting the group (Start with local businesses that are familiar to the women: salons, libraries, doctors' offices, and grocery stores. Ask to put up flyers or posters advertising the meetings. Local newspaper offices can be contacted to advertise your group. Some will give reasonable rates when meetings are held in churches.

3. Coordinates publicity campaign, which may include the following:

   - banners and yard signs
   - mass mailings and biweekly mailings
   - 3 × 5 promotion cards
   - free parent magazines
   - flyers to schools and businesses
   - church bulletins
   - website, Facebook

4. Keeps a time log of dates and businesses scheduled for advertising

5. Includes It's 4 uKids information in all church advertisements

6. Keeps a current mailing list based on the registration of women after the first meeting

☐ 1 Month Prior to the First Meeting

1. Follows up on the process of the advertisements of the moms' group (See point 2 of "3–4 Months Prior.")

2. Sets dates for the completion and delivery of banners and signs

☐ 2 Weeks Prior to the First Meeting

1. Contacts and follows up with advertisements (See point 2 of "3–4 Months Prior.")

2. Oversees the design of flyers and assists with the mailings

3. Repeats the process of biweekly mailings (current mailing list), church bulletins, website, Facebook

☐ 1 Week Prior to Each of the Meetings

1. Oversees the completion of all advertisements (See point 2 of "3–4 Months Prior.")

2. Corrects and completes all advertisements that have not been completed (See point 2 of "3–4 Months Prior.")

☐ 3–4 Days Prior to Each Meeting

Reports to coordinator or director regarding the completion of all advertisements

☐ Day of Each Meeting

1. Is available to assist coordinator or director with completion of any tasks before the meeting begins

2. Greets and meets moms arriving at the meeting (Leaders should greet guests separately, starting by opening the door or standing at the entrance and then scattering throughout the room. Discourage the group of leaders from greeting the attendees as a group, because there is a tendency to chat among themselves instead of greeting each woman as she enters the room.)

☐ After Each Meeting

1. Attends a short review meeting with the coordinator and director

2. Assists with cleanup

Table Leaders (2–10 Women)

Description

Each table leader must be a Christian mom, a member of the charter church, and someone who desires to build relationships with new moms and to have timely faith conversations. This position requires someone who can start conversations and ask questions of new guests so as to include them in the table talk. The goal of the table leader is to make the guests at her table feel important and comfortable, so they want to return and become a part of the moms' group.

Responsibilities

1. Greet visitors as they arrive. Leaders need to greet the moms separately, not as a group, so they can focus on each mom as she enters the room. A greeter can be at the door and open it for the mom. Other leaders can be around the room and greet all the moms before the meeting begins.

2. Contact women about the meetings.

3. Encourage the leaders to have a get together with community moms at times other than the regular meetings. Examples: playground time, birthday parties, and home visits.

4. Pray for each woman at her table.

5. Assist in reminder calls, sending cards, or other means of communication used to keep in touch with moms attending the meetings.

   - This leader may also be a supervisor, and a supervisor may also be a table leader.

   - The table leader will be a leader of a table that represents her oldest child. Depending on the size of your group, you may have designated seating for your guest and request they sit at the table that represents the age of her oldest child. Or, they can sit where ever they feel most comfortable. The moms' group can decide what works best for their group of moms.

- The table leader is the connecting link to reach community moms for Christ. They are the ones to build the relationships.

Timeline for Table Leaders

The timeline is important to follow so responsibilities are completed in a timely manner. In doing so, this leader can stay focused on opportunities that will come her way as she uses this ministry as a way to connect with community moms and, through her actions, show them Christ. The timeline will help accomplish this goal and keep everything in perspective.

☐ **3–4 Months Prior to the First Meeting**

1. Attends all required meetings designated by the coordinator

2. Prays for meetings, moms, and details of meetings

☐ **1 Month Prior to the First Meeting**

Assists with any projects the coordinator needs completed

☐ **2–3 Weeks Prior to the First Meeting**

1. Assists in distribution of flyers and advertising cards

2. Invites and does follow-up on all of the guests they have asked to attend.

- schools
- libraries
- grocery stores
- salons
- doctors' and dentists' offices

☐ **1 Week Prior to Each Meeting**

Assists coordinator with any projects or tasks that need to be completed by the meeting

☐ 3–4 Days Prior to Each Meeting

Continues to invite and follow up with moms, reminding them of the upcoming meeting via the following:

- Facebook or e-mails
- phone calls or text messages

☐ Day of Each Meeting

1. Contacts any mom who needs to be reminded or encouraged to attend the meeting

2. Arrives twenty minutes prior to time of meeting to greet moms as they arrive

3. Is available to assist in any task that needs to be done

☐ After Each Meeting

1. Thanks moms for coming and invites them to the next meeting (Each leader will thank the moms who are assigned to her table. It is a polite gesture to thank all visitors for coming. Each leader should thank the moms individually for attending.)

2. Attends a short review meeting with the director and coordinator after the moms have left

3. Helps with cleaning up their table areas and other cleanup tasks

Mentor Mom

Description

The mentor mom needs to be a mature, Christian mom whose children are grown, a member of the charter church, and someone who understands the importance of mentoring relationships. A woman who has already walked the mothering path can be a coach, guide, counselor, and prayer partner for young moms attending the meetings. Depending on the size of the group, there may be one or more mentor moms.

Responsibilities

1. Implement the Titus 2 woman.

2. Take responsibility for one table (exception would be if group is small enough to have only one mentor mom).

3. Pray for each woman for whom she is responsible.

4. Share ideas as needed.

5. Do the extras for her table, such as sending cards and making phone calls.

6. A designated mentor mom will give a five- to ten-minute devotional that goes with the theme of each particular meeting.

Timeline for the Mentor Mom

A timeline is important for this position because this individual needs to stay focused on the opportunities she has before her in mentoring and loving the women the Lord puts before her. The goal is to stay in touch with each woman assigned to her.

☐ 3–4 Months Prior to the First Meeting

1. Attends all required meetings designated by the coordinator or director

2. Starts a prayer list and prays for the needs of the meeting, the leaders, and the moms who will be contacted and invited to the group

3. If designated by the coordinator or director, acts as leader of the mentor moms if more than one mentor mom is assigned to the group

☐ 1 Month Prior to the First Meeting

Is available to assist the coordinator with any task that needs to be completed

- Assists with the mailing
- Assists with the distribution of flyers
- Assists with decorations for the meeting

☐ 2 Weeks Prior to Each Meeting

Contacts moms at their assigned table via the following:

- e-mail or Facebook
- phone calls or text messages
- notes in the mail: birthday, anniversary, thinking of you, and encouragement cards

☐ 3–4 Days Prior to Each Meeting

1. Assists the coordinator in the completion of tasks

2. Assists the table leader with anything that needs to be completed

☐ Day of Each Meeting

1. Assists the coordinator with any task that needs to be completed

2. Arrives twenty to thirty minutes prior to the meeting

   - Assists with any task
   - Greets moms as they arrive

☐ After Each Meeting

1. Thanks moms for attending the meeting and invites them to come to the next meeting (Thank women individually, and not as a group, so it gives a more personable touch.)

2. Attends a short review meeting with the coordinator and the director

3. Assists with cleanup

Schedule of It's 4 uMom Group Meeting

This schedule should be used as a guideline for It's 4 uMom group meetings. It may be adjusted according to the needs of each group.

10–15 Minutes: Greeting (Have each leader greet members individually. A person stays more focused on the visitor when greeting guests separately.)

5 Minutes: Early-bird drawing (The drawing should include the names of women who arrived early or on time. This is incentive for moms to arrive on time.)

3 Minutes: Welcome

10 Minutes: Icebreaker (coordinate with the speaker of the evening)

3 Minutes: Introduction of the pastor (first meeting only)

Pastor—Welcome and speaker introduction

20–25 Minutes: Speaker

20–25 Minutes: Refreshments (can be served before or after the speaker)

5 Minutes: Door prizes

5–10 Minutes: Mentor mom moment (object lesson with a spiritual lesson)

3–4 Minutes: Closing prayer

There would be no special music or group worship at the meeting. This is outreach and is geared to the community women, so you would not want to embarrass them in this setting.

Remember, it is all about them, not about us.

Community Speakers, Activities, and Topics

These speakers and activities are examples of the types of meetings a group can do. These speakers may or may not be available in your location. A group can add to activities that fit their particular group.

1. Pediatrician or General Practitioner: This is a good speaker to have sometime during the year. When doctors are at a meeting, they usually will agree to Q & A time for moms.

2. Executive Chef: This is an excellent person to invite to a meeting, because she or he can give cooking tips, suggestions for healthy food choices, and guidelines for creating good and creative menus.

3. Coupon Lady: Anyone in this category is a hit with moms. Moms are always looking for ways to save money for her family.

4. Fashion Coordinator: This is a fun time for moms to learn tips on caring for herself. She needs to be her best for her family, and fashion tips help moms have a more positive outlook on life.

5. Financial Counselor: Ways for a family to save money is in great need in today's world. Financial guidelines and tips are a plus for any mom.

6. Teacher or Principal: (appropriate age level of most moms)   Listening to and sharing time with a teacher are valuable activities for any parent with a child in school. Topics of interest include helping with homework, dealing with bullies, and handling peer pressure.

7. Gyminator: A gyminator can give exercise tips for babies to elementary-age children. This person can also share ideas for exercises moms can do with their children.

8. Time Management Consultant: A mom's job is 24/7. She needs to know how to accomplish everything expected of her as a wife and mom and still find some time for herself.

9. Heart Disease in Women: Heart disease is the #1 killer in women, so knowing how to care for your body is very important. A speaker in this

field can help moms learn to care for themselves so they can care for their families.

10. Nurse or Cancer Spokesperson: October is Breast Cancer Awareness month. It is a good time to have a nurse or cancer spokesperson speak to moms on the importance of checking their breasts and taking care of themselves.

11. Police/Safety Officer: This speaker is to remind moms of the importance of safety for their children. Whether a child is walking home from school, sleeping in his or her bedroom, or shopping with mom, child safety in and out of the home is a must.

12. Anchorwoman from TV Station: Depending on the group's location and the popularity of a celebrity such as this, a news anchor could be a drawing card to increase attendance. A specific topic for discussion would also affect attendance.

13. Thanksgiving Dinner for Mom: This could be the event that features the executive chef. He or she would come and give cooking tips on how to cook a turkey and how to cook for a large group. This is a time for moms to share what they are thankful for and for the group to grow closer.

14. Moms' Christmas Party: This is a great time to share the gospel of salvation with a group of moms. It will help women understand the real reason for the season. A great Christmas party is a wonderful time together.

15. Valentine Party: Moms need to know people care about them. This is a good time to show compassion for single moms. This can be one of the best attended meetings, because everyone wants to be loved. Any small gift for each mom is a token of appreciation.

16. Soup, Salad, and Slippers: This is a great night for moms to chill and get better acquainted with the other moms at their tables. There is no designated speaker for this event, so depending on the time of year that you do this event, consider using this time as getting to know the women who are assigned to a particular table. Women are to wear their slippers and bring their favorite soup or salad. The whole evening is spent chatting around the table and getting to know one another. This type of meeting is a good way to start the year. For example, if you start the meetings in the fall (September), the second meeting of the month is a good time to have soup, salad, and slippers.

17. Amazing Race and a Cookout: This is a fun night to watch moms in action. The leaders can set up a scavenger race. The women will be divided into small groups and will have to run all over campus, trying to find things. The group that first finds all the items on their list is the winner. Meanwhile,

the mentor moms are cooking hotdogs and hamburgers on the grill. This is a great spring event.

18. Award Night: This is the last meeting of the year. At the beginning of the year, the group can discuss a perfect attendance award—a challenge for table leaders to always have every chair at their table occupied by a mom. There can be awards given to the youngest mom, the mom with the most children, and so on. This is also a good time for table leaders to get contact numbers from their table group, so they can keep in touch during the summer.

Samples
for
It's 4 uMom

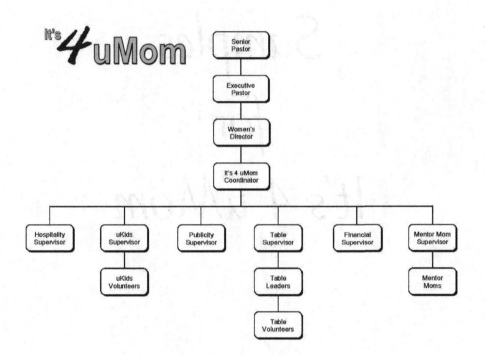

Timeline

Staff	3-4 Months	2 Months	1 Month	2 Weeks	3-4 Days	Day of	After Meeting
Pastor	Meets with the ladies of the church. Designates director.	At any given time the Pastor may meet with the director and/or coordinator and get reports.					
Director	Selects coordinator and meets with her and supervisors. Prays for leaders. Helps set speakers for the year.	Follows up with coordinator and supervisors on responsibilities. Checks on speakers.	Meets with coordinator and supervisors and gets Updated reports.	Meets with coordinator and supervisors and gets Updated reports. Touch base with speaker.	Contacts coordinator. Confirms speaker.	Checks with coordinator. Arrives 30 minutes prior. Greets speaker.	Thank yous. Clean up. Debrief with leaders.
Coordinator	Selects supervisors with director. Helps set speakers for the year.	Meets with director to appoint table leaders.	With director, writes schedule of meeting. Meets with supervisors and gets updated reports.	Meets with director and supervisors and gets updated reports.	Reviews schedule with director. Checks on supervisors.	Gives final report to director. Checks with supervisors. Arrives 30 minutes prior. Greets moms.	Thank yous. Closes in prayer. Clean up. Debrief with leaders.
Publicity	Attends meeting. Contact businesses to advertise. Assist in mass mailings.		Follows up on advertising. Completion of banners and signs.	Oversees design of flyer.	Reports completion of ads.	Assists where needed.	Clean up. Debrief with leaders.
Hospitality	Attends meetings.		Orders supplies.	Verifies receipt of supplies.	Delivers supplies and report to coordinator.	Assists with setup of décor and refreshments.	Thank yous. Clean up.
uKids Supervisor	Meets with volunteers. Oversees curriculum. Schedule and oversee supplies.		Meets with volunteers and designates specific responsibilities.	Double checks curriculum and supplies, room setup, etc.	Follows up with responsibilities of volunteers.	Arrives 30 minutes-1 hour prior. Places volunteers and greets moms and children.	Discusses results of evening with volunteers, clean up, and have prayer.
Table Leaders	Attend meetings		Assists with completion of projects.	Assist with distribution of flyers and cards.	Assist with projects. Invite and follow up with moms	Contact moms. Arrive 20 minutes prior.	Thank yous. Clean up. Debrief with leaders.
Mentor Moms	Attend meetings. Start prayer list.		Assist with mailings and flyers.	Contact moms by e-mail, face-book	Assist table leaders.	Arrive 20 minutes prior.	Thank yous. Clean up. Debrief with leaders.

Registration Form

Welcome to It's 4U Mom! Please complete this form so we can learn more about you!

Last Name: _____ First Name: _____ M.I. _____

Home Phone: _____ Alternate Phone: _____

Address: _____

City: _____ State: _____ Zip Code: _____

Neighborhood: _____
(Example: Across Street, Country Creek, and Marietta)

E-mail Address: _____ Birthday: _____

Facebook Name: _____

Have you attended a moms' group before? ☐ Yes ☐ No

If yes, where and what was the name of the group? _____

Home Church (if applicable): _____

How did you hear about It's 4U Mom? _____

Please list your child(ren)'s name(s) and age(s), listing oldest first:
Name: _____ Age: _____
Name: _____ Age: _____
Name: _____ Age: _____
Name: _____ Age: _____

Are you expecting, and if so, what is your due date? _____

Husband's Name (if applicable): _____

Are you interested in an age-appropriate playgroup for your child (children)? _____

If yes, can other moms contact you? _____

Our moms group is completely run by volunteers. If you are interested in volunteering in any of the areas below, please rank from 1 to 5 your volunteer preference. You will be contacted by a committee member with more information.

_____ Special Events   _____ Welcoming Committee   _____ Mailings/Website

_____ Activities   _____ Set Up/Tear Down   _____ Door Prizes

I would like more information about the following:
_____ Trinity Baptist Church

For It's 4U Mom Group Use Only

Date Registration Received:_____ Table Leader: _____

Letter to Local Businesses for Donations

To Whom It May Concern:

[Insert your church name here] is opening its doors to community moms to be a part of It's 4 uMom. This is a nonprofit organization geared to meet the needs of community mothers and their children.

We would like businesses in the area to participate through contributions, such as gift certificates, donations of paper items or decorations, or even sponsor a particular event for this group of moms. Any contributions your business can provide to make our meetings more successful in making better moms is greatly appreciated.

Thank you in advance for your contribution.

Sincerely,

Josie Aenis
Founder, It's 4 uMom
555-555-5555
josie@its4umom.com
http://www.its4umom.com

Volunteer Sign-Up for uKids

NAME	CELL PHONE	E-MAIL ADDRESS	FACEBOOK NAME

It's **4uMom** uKids Sign-In Sheet

Date_____Room_____

Child's Name	ID#	Birthday	Color of Bag	Name of adult Picking up child	Cell Number Please	Child's Allergies

WORKERS:
PLEASE SIGN IN: _____   _____

_____   _____

_____   _____

Revised August 2011

It's 4 uMom Master Attendance 2011-2012														
Name	9/12	9/26	10/10	10/24	11/7	11/21	12/5	1/9	1/23	2/6	2/27	3/12	3/26

It's 4 uMom Attendance 2011-2012

Table Leader: _____

Name	9/12	9/26	10/10	10/24	11/7	11/21	12/5	1/9	1/23	2/6	2/27	3/12	3/26

It's 4 uMom Leader's Attendance

Leader: _____

Name	9/12	9/26	10/10	10/24	11/7	11/21	12/5	1/9	1/23	2/6	2/27	3/12	3/26

It's 4 uMom Master Mailing List

Name	Address	City	State	Zip

It's 4 uMom

Building Relationships through Every Stage of Mothering

**Scavenger Hunt
&
A Minute to Win It!**

March 21, 2011

6:30–8:00 p.m.

Fellowship, Games, Door Prizes, Fun!!
Outdoor Cookout

Hot dogs/hamburgers will be provided!
Bring a friend and your favorite picnic dish!

Pizza will be provided for uKids (newborn–kindergarten).
Contact Josie Aenis at Josie@its4umom.com for further information.

It's 4 uMom

September 17

6:30–8:00 p.m.

Speaker:

Dr. Gene McConnell

Pediatrician at St. Vincent Hospital
"Responsible Parenting"
Coping with common behavior problems; spoiling: what it is and isn't

• There will be question and answer time

Early-bird door prize and refreshments
Bring a preschool mom
uKids: (newborns–kindergarten) free pizza

Contact: Josie Aenis Josie@its4umom.com

It's 4 uMom
"A Valentine for Mom"

February 7, 2011
6:30–8:00 p.m.

Special Guests:

Loved Moms

Fellowship, Games, Door Prizes, Fun, and Chocolate!!

Bring a *friend* and a *Valentine dessert* and join us in the Dining Commons. Pizza will be provided for uKids (newborn–kindergarten). Contact Josie Aenis at Josie@its4umom.com

Greetings from It's 4 uMom
@ Place Church Name Here

Newsletter
Summer 2011

It's hard to believe it's almost July, and we are about to celebrate Independence Day. We live in a great country and have a lot to be thankful for. Let's celebrate our nation's heritage and thank God for the wonderful blessing of Freedom!

Ongoing Local Events
Christian Music Night @ Skate Station
Thursdays, 7–9 p.m. $5
230 Blanding Blvd Orange Park

MOSH-Dinosaurs & Ice Age Mammals
Through October 14
Cummer Museum—Free on Tuesdays

Beat the Heat with a Free Movie

June 26 & June 27 Jonah: A Veggie Tale (G) or Garfield: A Tale of Two Kitties (G)

July 3 & July 4 Spongebob Squarepants (PG) or Jimmy Neutron: Boy Genius (G)

July 10 & July 11 Rugrats in Paris (G) or Ice Age: The Meltdown (PG)

July 17 & July 18 Flushed Away (PG) or Doogal (G)

July 24 & July 25 Everyone's Hero (G) or Racing Stripes (PG)

July 31 & August 1 Happy Feet (PG) or Rugrats: The Movie (G)

Regal Cinemas 904-992-4394 @ 14051 Beach Blvd. (Tues./Wed. 9:30 a.m.) or 904-538-3889 @ 9525 Phillips Highway (Wed./Thurs. 9:30 a.m.)

Josie's Helpful Hint for Tick Removal

Apply a glob of liquid soap to a cotton ball. Cover the tick with the soap-soaked cotton ball, and let it stay on the insect for fifteen to twenty seconds. The tick will come out on its own, stuck to the cotton ball.

Please consider yourself invited to our annual July 3 celebration, the Family Freedom Fest. Bring your family, friends, and neighbors: Everyone is welcome! We have motorcycle and car shows, rock-climbing walls, and inflatable fun stations for the kids! There will be plenty of food vendors. Bring blankets and lawn chairs, so you can relax and enjoy the spectacular fireworks show as the evening concludes.

⋏ **When**:   July 3, 2007, from 5 p.m. until dark and the fireworks!

⋏ **Where**:   The Central Campus (between the Auditorium and the Foundation).

⋏ **What**:   Food, Fun, and Fireworks

⋏ **Why**:   To come together with the people of our community to celebrate freedom in a safe and fun environment. Contact It's 4 uMom at josie@its4umom.com for resources.

Budget Guideline

This guideline can be adapted to meet the needs of individual groups.

The following are budget line items:

1. Room Decorations

   a. Tablecloths
   b. Centerpieces
   c. Room banner
   d. Door prizes
   e. Paper supplies

2. Advertising

   a. Banners
   b. Yard signs
   c. Mass mailing
   d. Flyers

3. Honorariums for Speakers

4. Child Care

   a. Supervisors
   b. Caregivers
   c. Supplies and crafts

A Prayer for Leaders

God, thank you that we can be involved in the lives of moms. Help us as supervisors to take our responsibilities as a special endeavor you have given to us. Help us to reach out and care for the needs of moms you bring our way. Help us to pray for our new friends, with whom we will be building relationships. May we realize this is not about us, and may these women see Christ in our walk and in our talk. Energize us, and may we win souls for your glory.

We ask this in Jesus' name.

Amen